Islam

& The Business Mind-Set

Day-to-day motivational tips
and advice for business owners

Copyright © Ilyas Salim, 2019 CE/1440 AH

Islam & The Business Mind-Set

Published by: Ta-Ha Publishers Ltd.
                                 Unit 4, The Windsor Centre
                                 Windsor Grove, London,
                                 SE27 9NT

Website: www.tahapublishers.com
E-mail: support@tahapublishers.com

Author: Ilyas Salim
Edited by: Yusuf Rowlands and Abdassamad Clarke
Typeset and cover deisgn by: Abdassamad Clarke

A catalogue record of this book is available from the British Library.

ISBN-13:   978-184200-164-6 (paperback)
Printed and bound by: IMAK Turkey

Contents

Our Lord, majestic is His remembrance and pure are His names, says:

"If only the people of the cities had had iman and taqwa, We would have opened up to them blessings from heaven and earth." (Surat al-A'raf 7:95)

And He, majestic is His remembrance, said:

"If only they had implemented the Tawrah and the Injil and what was sent down to them from their Lord, they would have been fed from above their heads and beneath their feet." (Surat al-Ma'idah 5:66)

He meant – and Allah knows best – if only they had acted upon that which was revealed in the Tawrah and the Injil and in this Qur'an they would have eaten from above their heads and beneath their feet, meaning – and Allah knows best – He would have bestowed the world upon them fully. (Yahya ibn 'Umar, Ahkam as-Suq)

Introduction

I NOTICED a lack of literature about being an entrepreneur and running businesses specifically aimed at Muslims that is easy to read and put into practice. In this day and age, reading is often limited to smart phones and Facebook posts, and not many people read large detailed books. I personally enjoy reading small, straight to the point books, where I can take action from bullet points. Hence, this book is designed to fill that gap in the market.

In writing it, I also wanted to benefit and motivate young entrepreneurs, as well as other business owners. Even if my book inspires one individual, I would say I've done a good job!

About the author

Ilyas Salim has had a successful career in business, healthcare and also in the education sector. He studied in various institutions around the world and specialises in Islamic Sciences and Business. He has successfully managed many companies and is also the MD of Salim Enterprise, which is a global investment company, and successfully manages Scent Salim and Bright Future. He has received many awards in various fields including healthcare, business and education, and is regarded as one of the top young entrepreneurs in the north of England. Scent Salim has become a global brand, participating in exhibitions worldwide and attracting customers from all over the UK and abroad to their Oud Store in Leeds.

Ilyas believes that making money is always secondary in any business; the priority is to provide a service. He gives advice to young entrepreneurs about how to manage time, business and life, as you will see later in this book, central to which is his contention that balance is the key. He always reminds them of the purpose of life and that is important to run a business according to what is correct, moral and ethical.

He has also been involved with many charitable organisations, including founding one of Gambia's largest orphanages which his team manage from West Yorkshire. He is in addition the editor of Al-Saboor magazine.

Business Mentality and Purpose

THESE ARE some tips for anyone wanting to start a new business or for an existing business owner.

1. Make profit a secondary aim

The first goal of a Muslim business should be to please Allah and establish a halal way of life. Seeking profit is not a bad aim, but it should be secondary.

The Prophet ﷺ said:

"Seeking lawful means (of earning your living) is obligatory after having fulfilled (other) obligations."[1]

By making Allah the goal, and implementing Islamic rules of honesty, truthfulness and good behaviour with customers then, insha'Allah, any Muslim business is bound to succeed.

2. Be truthful and honest

The Prophet Muhammad ﷺ has said that the honest and truthful

---

1   Al-Jami' as-Saghir

businessman will be in Jannah amongst the Prophets, the truthful and the martyrs.[2] Honesty and truthfulness are essential in any business, and when it comes to building a business, it means building a relationship of trust with customers, which cannot be achieved through lies and deceit.

The beloved Messenger ﷺ stressed the importance of fairness in business whilst reprimanding a dishonest tradesman:

"Whosoever deceives us is not one of us."[3]

3. Be open to scrutiny and criticism

While this may be a bitter pill to swallow, as Muslims we must be ready to have our product, service or business scrutinised. We will always improve by learning from our mistakes. This also indicates a willingness to work with the costumer. Remember, ultimately, we are all responsible to Allah. If a business is cheating, Allah will eventually expose those involved. Furthermore, a halal business is not just one person's profit-making machine, it is also an institution of the Muslim community. Therefore, it must ensure that it meets all the required standards, the most important of which are set by the Qur'an and Sunnah.

The Prophet ﷺ said, "The religion is nasihah." We said, "To

---

2   Tirmidhi, Hakim

3   Ibn Hibban

whom?" He ﷺ said, "To Allah, His Book, His Messenger, and to the leaders of the Muslims and their common folk."[4]

Giving **nasihah** to the Muslims in general means sincerely wanting the best for them and giving them advice. The Prophet ﷺ said, "The rights of a believer over a believer are six," and among them he mentioned "...if he asks you for advice you should advise him." Giving **nasihah** involves guiding them towards that which will put their affairs in order both in this life and the next. It also involves protecting them from harm, helping them in times of need, providing what is beneficial for them, encouraging them to do good and forbidding them from doing wrong with kindness and sincerity, and showing mercy towards them. Abdullah ibn Mas'ud reported:

"The Prophet ﷺ said, 'No one who has the weight of a seed of arrogance in his heart will enter Paradise.' Someone said, 'But a man loves to have beautiful clothes and shoes.' The Prophet said, 'Verily, Allah is beautiful and He loves beauty. Arrogance means rejecting the truth and looking down on people.'"[5]

Therefore based on the above hadith, a person should not reject criticism and advice from others out of arrogance and pride but should see it as being constructive criticism that will help him and his business to improve.

---

4   Muslim
5   Muslim

4. Be clean!

This is especially important for a grocery store or a takeaway, where the presence of animal blood is expected. Not being careful in this means not only losing customers, but also leaves the potential for causing them and you to become ill. The Prophet ﷺ said:

"Cleanliness invites towards faith and faith leads its possessor to Paradise."[6]

Cleanliness, by the way, does not just apply to those areas of the premises a customer will see, but also includes equipment and storage areas.

5. Aim for a higher goal

Don't just aim for one successful halal grocery shop in your chosen neighbourhood. Think big! Improve the inventory of your store, the types of items in it, and strive to find ways to improve service and profit margins. Also, look into the possibility of combining resources within the Muslim community or with other shareholders to expand the business. Doing this will also reduce overhead costs and, in the long run, the price of products for your consumers. We should always aim higher and higher.

---

6   Tabarani

6. Work with others in your market

Yes, this can be very difficult. Finger-pointing, accusations and nasty rivalry often characterise businesses aiming to market the same products. But this is not the way a Muslim economy should work. Brotherhood in the Ummah cannot be forgotten. Consider forming an association of Muslim retailers or distributors that can sit down together to share experiences, set standards and learn to cooperate. This cooperation will benefit everyone in the long run. Allah's Messenger ﷺ said:

"A Muslim is the brother of another Muslim, so he should not oppress him, nor should he hand him over to an oppressor. Whoever fulfils the needs of his brother, Allah will fulfil his needs. Whoever brings his brother out of discomfort, Allah will bring him out of the discomforts of the Day of Resurrection. Whoever screened a Muslim, Allah will screen him on the Day of Resurrection."[7]

"Whoever wishes to have his sustenance increased, and his life-span extended, let him respect ties of kinship."[8]

---

7   Bukhari
8   Bukhari, Muslim, Abu Dawud, Ahmad

7. Do not sell haram products

While there are more "Muslim" businesses sprouting up, not everything they sell is permitted by Allah. It is not difficult to find Muslim-owned businesses selling pork, alcohol, and certain magazines, etc., while selling halal meat at the same time. This requires effort on the part of Muslim business owners to wipe out what is haram and ensure that their businesses only deal with that which is halal. Selling halal will always bring blessings in the business and also in one's personal life.

Allah says:

"Say: 'I do not find, in what has been revealed to me, any food that is haram to eat except for carrion, flowing blood, and pork – for that is unclean – or some deviance which has been consecrated to other than Allah.'"[9]

"You who believe! wine and gambling, stone altars and divining arrows are filth from the handiwork of Shaytan. Avoid them completely so that hopefully you will be successful."[10]

When Allah prohibits something, it includes all aspects of it: using it, consuming it, trading with it and giving it as a gift to people.

---

9   Qur'an, 6:145
10   Qur'an, 5:90

Business Mentality and Entrepreneurship

While economists and statisticians might come up with all sorts of theories, I've got a different take. I don't think a lot of people understand the true meaning of the word **entrepreneur**. My go-to online dictionary describes an entrepreneur as: "a person who starts a business and is willing to risk loss in order to make money" or "one who organises, manages, and assumes the risks of a business or enterprise." Note the common key-words **business** and **risk**. If there's no real business or risk, you're not an entrepreneur.

"You will be tested in your wealth and in yourselves and you will hear many abusive words from those given the Book before you and from those who are idolaters. But if you are steadfast and have taqwa, that is the most resolute course to take."[11]

The commentators of the Noble Qur'an have said that the ownership of wealth and properties is man's in terms of benefit, trial and test. So, Allah the Almighty has granted you the ownership of money for you to benefit from it via profit, for example, and to be tested through it both in profit as well as loss and difficulties in business.

A true entrepreneur is ready to work hard, listen to elders and learn

---

11   Qur'an, 3:186

from his or her mistakes. To ensure we have a good understanding of going into any business deal, or even an investment or partnership, it is always important to understand the key risk factors.

The Risk Factors in Business

Let's have a look at five business risks:

Risk 1: Business interruptions. These are things such as a building catching fire, the illness of a team member and other unforeseen events, which can force vulnerable businesses to relocate or close.

Solution: Create a disaster recovery plan that includes data-backup and recovery strategies, as well as plans on how to set up in a different location and alert employees to what is going on. This helps cover your operating costs and loss of income so that you can help maintain payroll while you replace equipment and repair damage. Coverage typically provides reimbursement for up to a year of lost revenue.

Risk 2: Property loss. Your business property needs protection from the unexpected — just as your home does.

Solution: Audit your physical locations and business processes to identify and address areas of vulnerability.

Risk 3: Injury. Workplace injuries can result in medical treatment costs and lost productivity. They can also inflate business insurance premiums.

Solution: Educate employees about workplace safety and ensure that you have proper workers' compensation insurance in place. This insurance provides wage replacement and medical benefits to staff members who are injured on the job.

Risk 4: Liability. Liability companies are at risk of lawsuits for accidental injury, libel or slander and other unanticipated results of day-to-day business.

Solution: Carefully designed business practices can help mitigate risks, but it can be difficult to guard against unknown future events. General, product and professional liability policies offer coverage for businesses that are exposed to specific threats. These policies offer protection against third-party insurance claims. Talk to your insurance agent to see what kind of liability coverage your company may need.

Risk 5: Security breach. In today's digital world, businesses can be instantly crippled by a loss of data or data theft.

Solution: Map a strategy to help protect your company data both on-site and remotely. If it would be difficult for your business to recover from data loss, consider investing in data compromise and identity recovery insurance. This can help to protect against loss or damage to computer equipment, data storage devices, electronic information, software and expenses related to data recovery. Your insurance agent can help you find the right policy and determine appropriate coverage levels.

Yes, I know that ideally co-operative insurance is the route to go in order to comply with the shari'ah, but in the absence of that, it is simply inconceivable for most businesses once they reach a certain scale to do without insurance, and if the only available form is commercial then necessity is the deciding factor.

As a reader you probably don't want to hear this but if I don't tell you, who will? Being an entrepreneur is not a job. Being a leader is not a job. Being a social media guru is also not a job. If there's no real expertise, no real product, no real business, no real risk, and no real prospect for return on investment, you're not working, you don't have a job and you're not an entrepreneur either. If you want to be an entrepreneur someday, it is an equation you should print out and attach to your mirror, computer screen, smartphone, or wherever your eyeballs spend most of the time. Let's look at two examples.

Evan Spiegel is the CEO of Snapchat. That's his job. It's a real company with a real product, real employees, and real investors, and I bet what he really identifies with is the cool, fleeting messaging app the company he co-founded came up with, which is how they managed to attract hundreds of millions of extremely engaged users and raise more than half a billion dollars in venture funding.

John Mackey is co-CEO of Whole Foods. Healthy food has always been his passion but the way he built his company — to serve all its major stakeholders — is unique. He wrote a book about it called **Conscious Capitalism**. I seriously doubt that Mackey thinks of himself as a great entrepreneur, but as the co-founder of a great company that showed the world a new and better way to do business.

I could go on, but I think you get the point. These guys have jobs. Real jobs. They have products. Real products. And they have real companies that do real business. If you want to be a successful entrepreneur, don't start out wanting to be one. Start out with a customer problem and a product that solves it. Get capital. Make the product, market it, win customers. Someday you'll wake up and realise what you've become: a guy who took a risk, started a business and made money. An entrepreneur.

Why Open a Business?

ALLAH'S MESSENGER ﷺ was asked what type of earning is best and he ﷺ replied, "A man's work with his hand, and every business transaction which is approved."[12]

Why should you start a business? If you're an entrepreneur you have heard a million reasons not to go into business: it's too risky, you might get into debt, you'll probably lose sleep, your social life will be finished, and the list goes on. But even with all these uncertainties, people are still attracted to the start-up world. However, there are just as many, if not more reasons to take the leap and start your own business.[13] Here are just a few:

1. Spare time

Initially you'll work longer hours for less pay. But if you do it right, you could start to master your schedule, and the freedom that being an entrepreneur brings is awesome, freedom to observe the prayers and spend quality time with the family will be the greatest benefits to your life.

When you build something successful, it's an experience of

---

12 At-Tirmidhi
13 https://www.entrepreneur.com/article/235224

abundance. You had a vision, you were able to execute it and now can reap the benefits of saying, "I did this alhamdulillah."

2. Something for your posterity

If you're a doctor, plumber or bus driver, it's hard to imagine you passing your career on to your loved ones. But if you own your own business, it's something you can pass on to the next generation and be proud of it, because you created it.

3. Job security

Have you ever been laid off, downsized, or fired? If you have, you will get this. With entrepreneurship the security lies in the fact that you are your own boss; you run the show and don't have to worry about getting laid off.

4. Networking

Entrepreneurs are communal creatures. We love to meet each other, swap stories and learn from each other's experiences. Your circle of friends and acquaintances always grows when you become an entrepreneur, as we need others to lean on to survive, talking about the challenges only known to us.

5. Doing good to benefit others

While this isn't exclusive to entrepreneurs, it's definitely a perk. You control where your company profits go and, if you choose, you can allocate financial gains to others: you can sponsor a charity, a non-profit organisation or just personally give back to the community. This is quite honestly one of the best parts of being an entrepreneur.

6. Novelty

We humans love new experiences, and you can rarely experience a host of new things from inside your cubicle. This all changes when you are running the show. Starting your own business ensures that you're always facing challenges and experiencing something new.

7. Mentorship

Learning from masters and then helping those less experienced than you gives you a great sense of satisfaction. From my experience (and others' stories) the entrepreneurial community is very willing to give back and lend a helping hand.

8. Becoming an expert

This point goes along with mentorship. Regardless of what you do as an entrepreneur, if you stick with it, you'll probably become very good at it and this gives you a sort of soapbox — so use it. You'll have the chance to be interviewed for your expertise, to write about it and raise awareness of your message.

9. Skills

People often ask me how I learned about SEO (Search Engine Optimization; the process of getting traffic from the "free," "organic," "editorial" or "natural" search results on search engines), social media, pay-per-click, PR and all the other marketing techniques I utilise. The truth is I was forced to learn them in order to survive, the same way I was forced to learn how to build a spreadsheet, how to balance a budget, how to negotiate leases and countless other skills I picked up. I was the only resource I had. While developing new skills can be tough and takes time, it can pay off in **spades**. These skills will be invaluable throughout your life.

10. Determination

Everything I've done as an entrepreneur has affected me in my personal life. I used to be terrible at adapting to change. But being an entrepreneur for over a decade has forced me to become determined and dedicated to projects and causes; now I can actually stick to an exercise plan! I'm also better at being a father and a husband because of the determination I have learned.

11. Recognition

There are literally thousands of local, regional and national awards that recognise entrepreneurs in every field and industry. This shouldn't be your only reason to start a business, but it certainly is a great feeling when you receive it.

12. Financial independence

Let's be honest, this is probably the biggest reason people get into business for themselves, and that's a good thing! You **should** want financial independence. However you define financial independence — a retirement stockpile, unlimited cash potential or having the money to buy what you want — entrepreneurship can allow you to achieve it. Trust me, money doesn't buy happiness, but it can help in making life more comfortable along the way.

13. Reinvention

I've started and sold several companies over my career; every time I sell a company, I'm presented with an opportunity to reinvent myself all over again. On the flip side, if I had received my law degree, I'd be a lawyer (not a lot of room to recreate myself). As an entrepreneur, I get to be whatever I want to be.

14. Change the world

Everyone jokes that every entrepreneur says they're going to change the world. It's difficult to imagine how a mobile phone accessory stall in the mall is going to change the world, but there are those that do succeed. Take a look at Elon Musk, Bill Gates, Sergey Brin, and the countless other entrepreneurs who really have changed the world in some small (or major) way. But sometimes it's just about making a difference on a local or community level. The point is that you **can** make a difference in your own way.

15. Create jobs

There's nothing like the satisfaction of knowing you're responsible for the success of your employees. Your ideas provide them the opportunity to earn a living, provide for their family and fulfil their own dreams.

16. Your brand

Being known for something is awfully enjoyable. People may start referring to you as the marketing guy, or the retail expert or the software guru. Whatever it is you're recognised as — it's fun to build that brand and earn that recognition.

17. Your reason

I've given you a list of reasons why I think you should get into business. But all that really matters is **your** reason to start your own business. So, what is it?

Tips to Expand Your Business

REGARDLESS OF your definition of success, there are, oddly enough, a great number of common characteristics that are shared by successful business people. You can place a tick beside each characteristic you feel you possess. This way, you can see how you stack up. Even if you don't have all of these characteristics, don't fret. Most can be learned with practice and by developing a winning attitude, especially if you set goals and apply yourself, through strategic planning, to reach those goals in incremental and measurable stages.

The Home Business

Like any activity you pursue, there are certain essential qualities that are needed to be successful in any business. To legally operate a vehicle on public roadways, one must have a driver's license; to excel in sports, one must train and practise; to retire comfortably, one must become an informed investor and actively invest for retirement. If your goal is success in business, then the formula is no different. There are certain musts that have to be fully developed, implemented and managed for your business to succeed. There are many business musts, but this chapter contains what I believe to be some of the more important ones that are necessary to start, operate and grow a profitable home business.[14]

1. Do what you like doing

What you get out of your business in the form of personal satisfaction, financial gain, stability and enjoyment will be the sum of what you put into your business. So if you don't enjoy what you're doing, in all likelihood it's safe to assume that will be reflected in the success of your business — or subsequent lack of success. In fact, if you don't enjoy what you're doing, chances are you won't succeed.

2. Taking it seriously and professionally

You cannot expect to be effective and successful in business unless you truly believe in your business and in the goods and services that you sell. Far too many home business owners fail to take their own businesses seriously, getting easily side-tracked and not staying motivated and keeping their 'noses to the grindstone'. They also fall prey to pessimists who don't take them seriously because they don't work from an office building, office park, storefront or factory. Little do these sceptics know, who rain on the home business owner's parade, that the number of people working from home, and making very good annual incomes, has grown by leaps and bounds in recent years.

---

14   https://www.entrepreneur.com/homebasedbiz/index.html

3. Planning

Planning every aspect of your home business is not only a must, but also builds habits that every home business owner should develop, implement and maintain. The act of business planning is so important because it requires you to analyse each business situation, research and compile data, and make conclusions based mainly on the facts as revealed through the research. A business plan[15] also serves a second function: setting goals on paper and how they will be achieved. You can use the plan that you create both as a map to take you from A to Z and as a yardstick to measure the success of each individual plan or segment within the plan.

4. Character and Customer – the 2 C'S

Your home business is not about the products or services that you sell. Your home business is not about the prices that you charge for your goods and services. Your home business is not about your competition and how to beat them. Your business is all about your customers and clients; after all, your customers are the people that will ultimately decide if your business goes boom or bust. Everything you do in business must be customer-focused, including your policies, warranties, payment options, operating hours, presentations, advertising and promotional campaigns and websites. In addition,

---

15   https://www.entrepreneur.com/businessplan/

you must know who your customers are 'inside-out and upside down'.

5. Positive image

You have but a passing moment to make a positive and memorable impression on people with whom you intend to do business. Home business owners must go out of their way and make a conscious effort to always project the most professional business image possible. The majority of home business owners do not have the advantage of elaborate offices or elegant storefronts and showrooms to wow prospects and impress customers. Instead, they must rely on imagination, creativity and attention to the smallest detail when creating and maintaining a professional image for their home business.

6. Team

No one person can build a successful business alone. It's a task that requires a team that is as committed as you to the business and its success. Your business team may include family members, friends, suppliers, business alliances, employees, sub-contractors, industry and business associates, local government and the community. Of course the most important team members will be your customers or clients. Any or all may have a say in how your business will function and a stake in your business future.

7. Personal development

Top entrepreneurs buy and read business and marketing[16] books, magazines, reports, journals, newsletters, websites and industry publications knowing that these resources will improve their understanding of business, marketing functions and skills. They join business associations and clubs, and they network with other skilled business people to learn the secrets of their success and help define their own goals and objectives. Top entrepreneurs attend business and marketing seminars, workshops and training courses, even if they have already mastered the subject matter of the event. They do this because they know that education is an ongoing process. There are usually ways to do things better, in less time, with less effort and more efficiently. In short, top entrepreneurs never stop investing in the most powerful, effective and best business and marketing tools at their immediate disposal — themselves.

8. Have a Break

The temptation to work around the clock is very real for some home business owners. After all, you don't have a manager telling you it's time to go home because they can't afford the overtime pay. Every person working from home must take time to establish a regular work schedule that includes time to stretch your legs and take

---

16   https://www.entrepreneur.com/marketing/index.html

lunch breaks, plus some days off and scheduled vacations. Create the schedule as soon as you have made the commitment to start a home business. Of course, your schedule will have to be flexible. You should, therefore, not fill every possible hour in the day. Give yourself a backup hour or two. All work and no play makes you burn out very fast and grumpy customer service is not what people want.

9. Zakat and Business

Business assets are subject to Zakat and these include cash, finished goods, work in progress, raw materials and strong debts, i.e. money owed to the business that is likely to be received. Business assets must be valued at their current market price. For finished goods, this should be their retail sale price. For unfinished goods, this should be whatever price you expect the unfinished good to fetch on your Zakat anniversary date.

"O you who believe! Give from that which you have earned and from that which we have given you from the harvests of the land."[17]

Some narrations from the time of 'Umar ﷺ show that there was consensus among the Companions about the obligation of Zakat on business.

---

17   Qur'an, 2:267

The resources and fixed assets that are used by a business to run, such as a building, factory, warehouse, office equipment, IT systems, transport vehicles, etc. which are not directly for sale have no Zakat due upon them. Similarly, if an investment in the capital resources is made, such as renovations of the office – then this can be deducted from the wealth upon which Zakat is due.

The majority of scholars are of the opinion that the value of the commodity to be taken into account for Zakat purposes is the retail price and not the buying price. The price to take into account would need to be the wholesale price if most items sell wholesale, or retail pricing if most items retail.

Zakat that is levied upon businesses should be in the form of money and currency and not from the type of wealth that the business deals in – unless the poor need that type of wealth, in which case it would be permissible for the business to give the Zakat in terms of the commodity that it does business in.

Advice for Start-ups

MARKET RESEARCH should be an important part of a start-up's preparation and business planning; it helps to shape your marketing, resources and business plan and can influence how and who you plan to target, what pricing point you choose and it can even alter your business idea to become more profitable.

Fundamentally an effective research plan involves two elements: desk- and field-research.

How to do market research

Nowadays the internet and social media networks have had a huge impact on the development of market research practices, making desk research even more accurate and extensive. There is an ever increasing supply of secondary data available in published form, accessible either online or via business sections of public libraries throughout the UK and elsewhere, to enable both business startups and growers to quantify the size of market sectors they are entering and to determine trends in those markets.

However, the importance of going out into the field, speaking to customers directly, testing your product/service personally and building a brand through your interactions with users is still as important as it was prior to the evolution of data. This also entails getting out and finding out essential facts that have not been uncovered by desk research, either because the data hasn't been collected, or because it is deficient in some important aspect.

Very often, you will find that while general market information is available there is no specific information available for a particular town or region. Also, when the economic climate changes, say from boom to bust, buying patterns may shift quite suddenly, making desk research irrelevant. Here, we look at key areas of field research in order to help you plan and implement effective market research.

Observing your business's market

The importance of observation as a method of gathering data is accentuated because of the inconsistency between what people will say in an interview or in answer to a questionnaire, and what they actually do. It's not that people are necessarily lying, it's just that our capacity for self-deception is often high. Customers may feel foolish admitting they have difficulty understanding how to use a product or service, and so would not like to have that fact recorded. That doesn't mean that they don't have a problem, and a company would gain valuable information from finding out about it.

So, observation can give valuable insights into how things look to an outsider such as a customer, supplier or prospective employee. But such insights will only be representative of the time the researcher spent observing and may not be indicative of the general level of service. This type of research is often used to provide contextual information alongside other research methods.

Face-to-face interviews with your potential customers

Talking and listening to people is the most basic and the most used method of conducting qualitative research. Interviews differ from surveys; for example, they adhere less to a fixed set of questions but continually probe and cross-check information, building cumulatively on the knowledge gained from earlier answers.

Nevertheless, at some point interviewers have to ask questions that give them the specific data they need. Good interpersonal skills, sensitivity to the interviewee, conducting interviews at an appropriate time and place as well as choosing an appropriate sample of people to interview are all vital for success.

Focus groups

Focus groups are a form of interview with small groups of around eight to ten people who are selected with certain key attributes in mind, for example, specific knowledge, experience and/or socioeconomic characteristics. Participants are invited to attend informal discussion sessions of no more than two hours' duration on a particular topic.

Holly Tucker, our 2013 Golden Gun[18] and founder of successful online store 'Not On The High Street', says that arranging focus groups will help an entrepreneur see where their start-up will fit into the market and, with the right responses, can validate their idea:

"See enough people with a problem and you have a business opportunity. Working in the events and shopping sectors we realised there was a wealth of quirky and distinctive retailers without an affordable and effective method of selling their products."

Most of these businesses did not have an online presence and, of the ones that did, there were virtually none who had an e-commerce capability.

"The businesses we spoke to were desperate for what we were offering: a way of reaching customers without lugging their products around the country attending really expensive trade fairs which could cost thousands to exhibit at."

18   http://startups.co.uk/young-guns/notonthehighstreet-coms-holly-tucker-mbe-named-keystone-law-golden-gun-2013-young-guns/

For more basic research decisions on product design, pricing and packaging, for example, focus groups are used extensively by most of the major consumer brands. The advantages of using them include efficiency, as you can get ten opinions in around twice the time it takes to conduct a single interview, and often, by listening to other people's comments, more ideas, opinions, experiences and insights can be gained. It is also easier to take notes of a discussion than an interview, as this is expected and less threatening in a group situation. But, as with interviews, focus groups rely on the views of a small sample and so are not necessarily truly representative of any body of opinion.

The market research survey

The most common field research method is the survey. This is a near-ubiquitous tool used by organisations to get a handle on almost everything, from measuring market potential and assessing customer satisfaction to getting insights into almost any issue surrounding a product or service.

Around half of all surveys are conducted face to face, which is considered best for tackling consumer markets. Next in popularity come telephone, email and web surveys, which work well with companies and organisations. Postal surveys, once very popular, now account for less than 10% of survey work.

Interviewing requires a very positive attitude, courtesy and an ability not to talk too quickly and to listen while sticking rigorously to the questionnaire. Personally addressed email questionnaires have secured higher response rates, as recipients have a greater tendency to read and respond to email received in their private email boxes. However, unsolicited emails ('spam') will usually be ignored. The keys to success are an explanatory letter and incentives for the recipient to 'open' the questionnaire, and keeping the number of questions to a minimum, making them simple, and having an identifying question to show the cross-section of respondents and look for factual answers.

Just asking any person you come across questions is unlikely to give you reliable information. Unless you put some basic statistical method into your research you will be largely wasting time and money. You may also find that anyone reading your business plan or listening to your presentation will be underwhelmed if you can't explain how you went about gathering your data.

It isn't usually possible or even desirable to include every possible customer or competitor in your research. Instead you should select a sample of people who represent the whole population being surveyed. Sampling saves time and money and can be more accurate than surveying an entire population.

There are two main methods of sampling that can help ensure you have a population that will provide reliable data: **probability sampling**, which follows statistical rules with each member of the sample population having a known chance of being selected, and **non-probability sampling** which includes such methods as calling for volunteers or on-the-street interviews and using students as guinea pigs in an experiment.

This method can be further refined by selecting people or groups of people that you believe will result in a group that is representative of the population as a whole. Further refinement can be applied to ensure the people sampled represent the overall population in some important respect. For example, if we know that 60% of pet owners are women, then we might construct our sample with that proportion of women in it.

Testing the market

The best form of market research is to find real customers to buy and use your product or service before you spend too much time and money in setting up. The ideal way to do this is to sell to a limited area or small section of your market. In that way, if things don't quite work out as you expect you won't have upset too many people.

This may involve buying a small quantity of the product, as you need to fulfil the order to fully test your ideas. Once you have found a number of people who are happy with your product, price, delivery/execution, and have paid up, then you can proceed with a little more confidence than if all your ideas were merely just on paper.

Pick potential customers whose demand is likely to be small and easy to meet. For example, if you are going to run a bookkeeping business, select five to ten small businesses from an area reasonably close to home and make your pitch. The same approach would work with gardening, baby-sitting or any other service-related venture. It's a little more difficult with products, but you could buy a small quantity of similar items from a competitor or make up a trial batch yourself.

Nick Jenkins emphases the importance market testing had in Moonpig's creation:

"During my last weeks at Cranfield I took my idea to Paperlink, a successful greeting card publishing company without an online presence, and offered them a small stake in the company if they would let the as-yet-unnamed company use their greetings cards. Miraculously, they agreed, and this was enough to convince me I had an idea worth pursuing."

Market research will benefit your business on many levels, helping you get your business idea out there as well as gaining reliable data to include in your business plan.

Working smarter not harder

IN THIS day and age we have to keep up with trends in business, stay with people who will add value to you, go to business people for advice and ask them questions and learn from these people. In one of my favourite books,[19] Stephen Covey tells the story of a woodcutter whose saw becomes blunter as time passes and yet he continues cutting down trees. If the woodcutter had stopped sawing, sharpened his saw, and had gone back to sawing the tree with a sharp blade, he would actually have saved time and effort in the long run.

The analogy is an easy one to remember but harder to put into practice. Here's what Covey says about sharpening the saw in your life:

"Sharpen the Saw means preserving and enhancing the greatest asset you have: you. It means having a balanced program for self-renewal in the four areas of your life: physical, social/ emotional, mental and spiritual."

Sharpening the saw is a great habit to get into in all areas of your life, but I think it can be especially beneficial when it comes to work and helping you avoid burnout.

---

19   https://www.stephencovey.com/7habits/7habits-habit7.php

1. Take breaks

On average, your brain is able to remain focused for only 90 minutes, and then you need at least 15 minutes of rest (The phenomenon is based on ultradian rhythms[20]). By taking breaks approximately every 90 minutes, you allow your mind and body to renew – and be ready to fire off another 90-minute period of high activity.

For some people, 15 to 20 minute breaks might be tough to pull off, but taking short breaks throughout the day can still help you to refresh your mind and reset your attention span.[21]

2. Take naps

Research shows that naps lead to improvement in cognitive function, creative thinking and memory performance. In particular, napping benefits the learning process[22] by helping you take in and retain information better.

The improved learning process comes from naps actually helping

---

20 http://instituteforleadershipfitness.com/2012/05/peak-performance-and-the-ultradian-rhythm/
21 http://blog.bufferapp.com/the-science-of-focus-and-how-to-improve-your-attention-span
22 http://blog.bufferapp.com/novelty-and-the-brain-how-to-learn-more-and-improve-your-memory

your brain to solidify memories.[23] According to Gawker editor-in-chief Max Read, "Research indicates that when memory is first recorded in the brain — in the hippocampus, specifically — it's still 'fragile' and easily forgotten, especially if the brain is asked to memorise more things. Napping, it seems, pushes memories to the neocortex, the brain's 'more permanent storage', preventing them from being 'overwritten'.

One study[24] into memory found that following a nap participants did remarkably better in a test than those who didn't sleep at all. Not only are naps beneficial for consolidating memories and helping you remember new information (handy if your job includes a lot of research during the day!), they're also useful in helping you avoid burnout,[25] since research shows that burnout is a signal that you can't take in more information in this part of your brain until you've had a chance to sleep.

3. Spend time in nature

Daniel Goleman, author of **Focus: The Hidden Driver of Excellence,** suggests spending time in nature to help you reset your attention span and relax your mind. One experiment he mentions tested how relaxed people were when taking a walk down a city

23   http://gawker.com/5741490/want-to-memorize-something-take-a-nap
24   http://gawker.com/5741490/want-to-memorize-something-take-a-nap
25   http://news.sciencemag.org/2002/05/power-napping

street versus in a quiet park. The study found that the level of attention needed to navigate a busy city street is high enough that the walk doesn't let the brain relax[26] enough to reset your focus level:

"Unlike natural environments, urban environments are filled with stimulation that captures attention dramatically and additionally requires directed attention (e.g., to avoid being hit by a car), making them less restorative."

Spending time in nature, however, allows your mind to relax fully and unwind and helps you focus longer when you return to work. Plus, other research[27] has found that, for students, motivation to learn is higher when they are outside instead of in a classroom.

4. Move and work in blocks

I recently read a blog post[28] by Joel Runyon[29] about a method he calls "workstation popcorn". The idea is that you set up at various cafés or other workspaces to get chunks of work done throughout the day. Workstation popcorn starts with a clearly thought-out to-do list: You create a plan for what you will accomplish at each location so you can immediately jump into those tasks.

---

26 http://www.umich.edu/~jlabpsyc/pdf/2008_2.pdf
27 http://www.seer.org/pages/research/AthmanandMonroeJIR2004.pdf
28 http://impossiblehq.com/workstation-popcorn
29 http://impossiblehq.com/author/joel

Runyon breaks up his to-do list into sections – one per café that he plans to visit and each section into three clear tasks. Once he gets through the group of tasks he has set, he moves on to the next café on his list. Of course, you can sort out your task list however suits you best, but the important part to note is having a clear finishing point **based on your task list** rather than the **time** you will move to a new location. And when you move, cycling or walking is a good way to go, according to Runyon, who recommends taking a break away from work for at least 30 minutes.

I know entrepreneurs who often find this break period helpful for thinking through what they are working on or what they will do next." I know entrepreneurs who often find this break period helpful for thinking through what they are working on or what they will do next. Runyon also noted in his post that since he started this process he has been more productive and more active during the day, working fewer hours.

5. Check your email first thing

This one is fairly counter-intuitive: basically everyone says not to check email right away, but I do and find it extremely useful. Here are some ways checking email first helps me to be more productive during the day.

If you work in a remote team, a business trend that is increasingly common,[30] you'll know what it's like to have half of your team (or more) working while you're asleep. If you need to work closely with others, it's important to check in before you start your workday and make sure you're on the same page as everyone else.

Since I started working at Buffer,[31] I've woken up to emails saying I had typos to fix, a new blog post published, and even that Buffer had been hacked.[32] Dealing with important issues first thing helps me quickly make decisions about whether my day needs to be adjusted to fit in with what everyone else is doing or whether I can proceed with the tasks I already had planned.

Simple things make a big difference!

30   http://online.wsj.com/news/articles/SB10001424127887324539404578342503214110478

31   http://bufferapp.com/

32   http://open.bufferapp.com/how-being-hacked-impacted-our-startups-key-metrics/

Barakah and Blessings

What is Barakah?

"BARAKAH IS a term that means 'increase' and 'growth' and also 'happiness'. It is the establishment of divine goodness in something; from whence it exudes cannot be sensed by people, nor can it be outwardly quantified, nor is it limited by anything, but rather, something with Barakah in it is called Mubarak, and has an unexplainable increase and benefit in it from Allah."[33]

Having more barakah in your wealth does not mean the dollar amount increases, but rather that the benefits seen from that limited amount increase, reach further and last longer. Barakah in anything, especially wealth, which is a part of your destined sustenance from Allah Most High, can increase and decrease depending on the good and bad actions you do.

The Means of Bringing Barakah into Your Wealth and Life

There are many, many different means we can take to bring barakah into our wealth, and indeed into every aspect of our lives. The most

---

33   al-Isfahani, Mufradaat al-Qur'an

important thing to remember is that these are only means — worldly causes that we put forth with our human efforts — but the One who gives wealth and bestows blessings in the first place is Allah the Most High. Hence, these actions are not mathematical formulae for automatic increase. We must keep Allah at the forefront of our seeking in this world, and make pleasing and reaching Him the ultimate goal, rather than the increase of wealth. Amongst the things that bring about barakah are:

1. Earn a lawful (halal) and wholesome income

Ensure that your line of work does not contravene the Sacred Law and that your wealth is lawful. This not only includes what work you do, but who you work for and their source of income as well. Ensure that your work is ethical and moral.

2. Work with excellence, loyalty and honesty

Do not take a single penny that you do not duly deserve. Do not squander the time and resources that your employer is paying for. Be loyal and honest at work. Nothing reduces barakah like cheating or deception in a sale, or unethical practices like bribes.

"Someone who has no trust has no faith, and someone who does not fulfil his promises has no religion."[34]

---

34   Ahmad

3. Make a good intention for Allah's sake

Make your intention in earning to do so purely for Allah's sake, to provide for your family, to not have to borrow and ask from others, and to do good works for others.

"Actions are according to intentions, and everyone will get what he intended."[35]

4. Avoid riba/usury in all its forms, as much as possible

This includes receiving it, or paying it. If you must pay it due to a debt, work as hard as possible to pay it off in a short time then decide not to enter into it again.

"The Messenger of Allah ﷺ cursed someone who consumes riba, someone who pays it, someone who records it and the two who witness it, and he said: they are all the same."[36]

5. Give thanks for what you have been given

Allah Most High says in the Qur'an:

"And if you all give thanks [to Me, for what I have bestowed on you], I shall surely increase you."[37]

---

35 Bukhari
36 Muslim
37 Qur'an 14:7

Thank Allah with your tongue, your heart, by using His blessings for good purposes and by obeying and worshipping Him.

6. Give in charity, both yourself and your spouse

This includes obligatory charities (**Zakat, Sadaqat ul-Fitr** and the **Qurbani** for those with sufficient wealth), but also optional charity to good causes. The Prophet ﷺ said:

"Charity does not reduce wealth."[38]

The physical amount outwardly decreases, but the remaining amount attracts barakah so that the actual benefit from it is not less.[39]

7. Be God-conscious and increase in piety

Allah Most High says:

"Whoever is conscious of Allah, He makes a way out [of any difficulty] for them and provides them with sustenance from where they cannot conceive."[40]

8. Place your full trust in Allah Most High

Know that Allah is providing for you and sustaining you at each

---

38 Muslim
39 al-Nawawi, Sharh Muslim
40 Qur'an, 65:2-3

moment. Do not constantly worry, for this is from the Shaytan who tries to instil fear of poverty, whereas Allah offers bounties.[41] Allah says,

"…and whosoever puts their full reliance on Allah, then He is sufficient for them."[42]

9. Establish the prayer in your home

Work to establish the obligatory prayers amongst your family, and encourage extra optional **(nafilah)** prayers as well.[43]

"Instruct your family to do salat, and be constant in it. We do not ask you for provision. We provide for you. And the best end result is gained by taqwa."[44]

10. Read Qur'an in the home

In particular, reading Surah al-Waqi'ah in a house is known to prevent poverty. It is reported that the Prophet ﷺ said:

"Indeed, the house in which the Qur'an is recited, goodness [in it] increases…" and in another version, "things are made easier for its family."[45]

---

41   Qur'an 2:268
42   Qur'an 65:3
43   al-Biqa'i, Tafsir
44   Qur'an, 21:132
45   Ibn Kathir, Tafsir

11. Be generous and give gifts

This means giving people around you things that they love, from the things that you love. Start with your immediate family, relatives and neighbours. Become more generous and open-handed, and try to fight the urge to be stingy. The Prophet ﷺ said:

"Exchange gifts, as that will increase your love for one another."[46]

12. Be obedient, dutiful and respectful to your parents

This is a means of increase in one's lifespan and sustenance.[47]

13. Keep up family ties and be good to relatives

It is mentioned that there is barakah in the act of joining ties with family and relations, only when combined with piety and fearing God.[48]

14. Do not lie or make false oaths[49]

"So refrain from the filth of the idols and refrain from false words."[50]

---

46 Bukhari
47 al-Sha'rani, Lawaqih al-Anwar al-Qudsiyya
48 Ibn Hibban,
49 Ibn Hajr, Fath al-Bari
50 Qur'an, 22:30

15. Give a little more than what you owe when selling or paying someone[51]

16. Try to work starting in the early part of the day

Preferably, try to become productive after Fajr and do not sleep after sunrise. Try to make the most of working in the mornings, as the Prophet ﷺ said:

"O Allah, give barakah to my Ummah in their early-mornings."[52]

17. Eat together

The Prophet ﷺ said:

"Gather together to eat your food, and say Allah's name over it (i.e. say Bismillah) and you will be blessed in it,"[53] and "Eat together, all of you, and do not separate individually, because the barakah is in the group."[54]

18. Invite the pious to eat from your food

The Prophet ﷺ made du'a for the host from whose food pious people eat, as it attracts barakah. It also promotes good company

---

51   al-Munawi, Sharh Fayd al Qadeer
52   Ibn Majah
53   Abu Dawud
54   Ibn Majah

and changes the atmosphere of the home.[55]

19. Continuously ask Allah for forgiveness

Ask Allah's forgiveness often in your home and elsewhere by saying **"astaghfirullah** – I seek the forgiveness of Allah."[56]

"I said, 'Ask forgiveness of your Lord. Truly He is Endlessly Forgiving. He will send heaven down on you in abundant rain and reinforce you with more wealth and sons, and grant you gardens and grant you waterways.'"[57]

20. Be easy-going, of kind nature, and forgiving to others

This includes your spouse and family, and even those who wrong you. This should spur you to heal relations with anyone you or your family may have a rift with.[58] Aisha ﷺ reported that the Messenger of Allah ﷺ said:

"O Aisha, Allah is gentle and He loves gentleness. He rewards for gentleness with that which is not granted for harshness and He does not reward anything else like it."[59]

---

55 al-Bayhaqi, Sunan al-Kubra

56 al-Bayhaqi, Shu'ab al Imaan

57 Qur'an, 71:10-12

58 al-Munawi, Fayd al-Qadeer

59 Muslim

21. Do not be wasteful and extravagant, nor overly-attached to worldly things

This includes finishing all of one's food and living in moderation.[60]

"And do not be extravagant. Surely, Allah does not like the extravagant."[61]

22. Finally, ask Allah Most High to bless you with wealth

When the Prophet ﷺ was asked to pray for young Anas ؓ the first thing he prayed for was wealth.[62] Ask Allah to put the wealth in your hand, but not in your heart.

There are countless more ways to attract **barakah** into your life and earnings that are mentioned in the vast Islamic primary sources, as well as among the wisdoms of scholars and the righteous. We will suffice with what has been mentioned above.

The Reality of Financial Difficulties

When a Muslim's finances are tight, this is a test from Allah Most High. It is a mercy in disguise because, through something as worldly as wealth, Allah causes us to turn towards Him in earnestness. It

---

60 ibid.
61 Qur'an, 6:141
62 Bukhari

teaches us patience and contentment and results in forgiveness of our wrongdoing and in our reliance on Allah.

However, the general rule of thumb to attract blessings is always the same: When we attach our hearts to Allah Most High and submit to Him completely, and make Him our sole goal and purpose and not the blessings, then the barakah will enter our lives from all sides without us having to worry about it.

Sunnah Tips

EVERYONE KNOWS starting a business is heavily endorsed in the Sunnah and it is also the second biggest dream after owning a house and having a great balance in life.

A start-up can be a roller-coaster ride, which at best can be the top of the world and at worst can be very difficult.

I will share a few narrations of the Prophet Muhammad ﷺ which have benefited me a lot. Many people came to me over the years for advice on starting a business, and I was happy to share these narrations with them.

The Prophet ﷺ said: "An honest and truthful businessman will be in the shade of the throne of Allah."[63]

The Prophet Muhammad ﷺ has said that whoever buys stolen goods, knowing such goods to have been stolen, becomes a party to the act of theft.[64]

Almighty Allah's mercy descends on one who is gentle at the time

---

63   Isbihani
64   Tirmidhi

of buying, selling and requesting payment.[65]

Our Prophet Muhammad ﷺ has said that Almighty Allah proclaims: "I am the third partner of a two man partnership until one of them acts dishonestly to his partner, and, in such event, I then leave them."[66]

Prophet Muhammad ﷺ said that whosoever sells a defective product without disclosing its defect to the purchaser, shall earn the permanent anger of Almighty Allah and that the angels continuously curse such a person.[67]

Our Prophet Muhammad ﷺ has exhorted that we should refrain from taking oaths unnecessarily, for, although it helps in the sale of one's products, it reduces the blessings.[68]

Our Prophet Muhammad ﷺ has said, "Whosoever accepts returned products, Almighty Allah will wipe-out his punishment."[69]

We understand that Halal business in Islam is a fundamental element of the faith in regards to having financial freedom. It isn't essential however it is encouraged for Muslims to become

---

65   Tirmidhi
66   Abu Dawud
67   Ibn Majah
68   Bukhari
69   Muslim

entrepreneurs. Halal and haram business transactions need to be taken into consideration also when undertaking business transactions or operations.

Balance in Life

FOR MANY people, work-life balance is at best a good idea, or at worst a terrible modern day joke that doesn't make anyone laugh anymore.

Boris Groysberg and Robin Abrahams, wrote in an article for the Harvard Business Review (March, 2014) that "today's senior executives will tell you that 'Work/life' balance is at best an elusive ideal and at worst a complete myth." The underlying reason for this elusiveness is that we're connected and expected to be present both for "work" and "life" at all times; when we are at work, we're expected to be reachable by family and friends, and when we are at home we are expected to be on call for work and clients.

Despite the efforts of many companies to implement work-life balance practices for their employees, it is the individuals themselves who struggle most with juggling their roles in a meaningful and effective way.

As part of my work to develop faith-driven professional training for individuals and corporates, I looked into the life and sayings of the Messenger of Allah ﷺ and tried to extract practical lessons that would be beneficial for the modern day professional. Before we delve into these insights, let us explore five reasons why work-life balance is so hard to master.

Why is Work-Life balance so hard to achieve?

Listed below are five challenges that imperil the work-life balance:

1. It's subjective

Modern day work-life balance is based primarily on expectations. Is an executive who works 50—60 hours per week but makes it a point to be home for dinner at 6pm every evening considered to have "mastered" the work-life balance? Perhaps, from the executive's point of view, he might be proud of himself for being home for dinner every night, but his spouse or children might not appreciate that work occupies 80% of his time.

Similarly, consider the case of a working mother, who's torn between career and family. Who decides if she has achieved a work-life balance?

2. It's transient

The work-life balance is not fixed. It changes with seasons and with every stage of our lives. You may be able to achieve some form of balance when you have one child, you're junior staff, and you don't have many responsibilities. However, trying to achieve a work-life balance with three children, a demanding job, a mortgage to pay off, and being involved in so many other extra-curricular activities really is a challenge.

3. It's not measurable

How do we even begin measuring the work-life balance? Is there a metric or scoring system that tells us how well we're doing on the continuum? Are the number of hours spent on family vs. work vs. personal activities sufficient to measure our effectiveness in that? What about the quality of those hours? These questions and more make the debate even more difficult to resolve.

4. It emphasises 'work' as larger than life

The whole idea that there's 'work' and then there's 'life' is problematic on many levels. First, it assumes that work is the centre of our lives and everything else is peripheral. Second, it assumes that work can never be integrated into life and that there's a 'Great Wall of China' separating the two.

As Dr. Stewart Friedman argues in his book, **Leading the Life You Want: Skills for Integrating Work and Life**, the idea that 'work' competes with 'life' ignores the more nuanced reality of our humanity, which is arguably the interaction of four domains: work, home, community and the private self. The goal needs to be to create harmony between these four areas instead of thinking only in terms of trade-offs.

5. It's hard to plan for

Let's be honest: you can plan the most balanced lifestyle, giving due time to every role you have, but reality always wins. Whether it's that last minute emergency meeting at 4pm that disturbs your dinner plans, or rushing to the hospital in the middle of a client meeting because your child had an injury at school — life keeps throwing stuff at us that makes it impossible for us to manage and truly have a balanced lifestyle.

By now, you might be thinking that achieving a work-life balance is totally unattainable! It's the right time to consider some insights from our Prophet Muhammad's life and practices ﷺ.

Three key lessons from the Prophet Muhammad ﷺ that help solve the above challenges

When one observes the daily routine of the Messenger of Allah[70] ﷺ, one cannot help but notice how balanced and effective it was. This is the man who, in just 23 years changed the face of humanity with his mission. Interestingly, we never hear complaints from his family or Companions that "he was too busy" or "didn't have enough time for us."

---

70   http://productivemuslim.com/daily-routine-of-prophet-muhammad/

Although some might think that the Prophet did not have a 9–5 job or experience the demands of the modern world, he was fully occupied day and night 24/7 with the wider community and his family, which was much larger than any of ours, experiencing far more numerous and greater challenges than we have. An enormous amount of what he did and said was recorded for posterity as an example for coming generations. Thus we can extract key lessons from his life that are applicable for us today.

1. Scrap the work-life balance and focus on total life balance

The Prophet once heard that one of his Companions was fasting every day and spending all night in prayer. He made a point to go and visit him and advise him not to do this. Here's what he told him:

> "…I have been told that you stand all night (in prayer) and fast all day.' I said: 'Yes (I do).' He said: 'Do not do that. Sleep and stand (in prayer), fast and break your fast, for your eyes have a right over you, your body has a right over you, your wife has a right over you, your guest has a right over you and your friend has a right over you…'"[71]

What fascinates me about this incident is that the Prophet

---

71   an-Nasa'i, 2391

made a point to go and visit the man and advise him to stop. All of this despite the fact that the man was engaged in devotional acts of worship, which one would have thought the Prophet ﷺ would be pleased about.

The key lesson for us here is that, instead of thinking of work-life balance in terms of what others expect from us, we should think of it in terms of fulfilling rights: the rights of our body, the rights of our mind, the rights of our families, the rights of our friends and, of course, the rights of our workplaces.

Once we shift our thinking of work-life balance from subjective/idealistic notions to seeing it from the point of view of the rights of others (& ourselves) it becomes intuitively very clear where to draw the line between the different parts of our lives and how to balance our lives given the circumstances. The elegance of this is that it takes away the guilt normally associated with the work-life balance. For example, if we know that we've fulfilled the rights of our workplace, then we shouldn't feel guilty if we leave at 5pm just because everyone else expects us to stay longer.

To implement this lesson in practice, we need first to identify the different roles that we play in our lives and then understand what rights each of these roles/entities have upon us. For example, as Muslims, one area for which we need to 'shepherd our time' is in order to fulfil our responsibility of salat — this in itself is often a challenge, and many of us become chronically late for salat due to hectic workdays, commutes, meetings and lessons.[72] .

2. Quality time

There's a long narration in the books of hadith that I have only recently understood. It describes how Aisha ﷺ recounts a conversation with the Prophet ﷺ about eleven women who tell each other about their husbands' qualities. Aisha ﷺ tells about each of the eleven women and recounts in detail what each of them said. The last story is about a woman called Umm Zar who described her husband in positive terms and had no complaints about him, to which the Prophet ﷺ said: "I am to you as Abu Zar was to his wife Umm Zar."[73]

I used to scratch my head and try to understand the point of this narration. It made no sense to me until recently. There are various lessons to learn here, but the main point of this story has been for me to showcase how attentive the Prophet ﷺ was to his family, how present he was with them and what a good listener. Something as small as just taking time to listen to your spouse can have a massive impact on nurturing and restoring balance to your relationship. When

---

72 http://productivemuslim.com/chronically-late-for-salah/
73 Bukhari

it comes to achieving a total life balance, a lot of the time the small things are, in reality, the big things.[74]

Sometimes, when we talk about work-life balance, we tend to think of how much time we're spending at home, at work or with our friends. But if we are 50% at home (mentally) when we are at work, and 50% at work (mentally) when we are at home, then it is no wonder we constantly feel stressed and unable to keep up.

The ability to be focused and 100% engaged in everything they do is a key characteristic of successful leaders, who showcase how important the people around them are. When such leaders do become busy, the people around them know it is an exception, not a rule, and are understanding and compassionate towards them.

Work-life balance may seem elusive to many people, yet if we apply the key lessons above, like shifting the narrative around work-life balance to the fulfilment of rights and responsibilities, especially being present with those around us, we'll make huge strides in achieving a holistic, whole-life balance.

---

74   http://productivemuslim.com/dont-stop-being-kind/

Conclusion

BUSINESS HAS always been an essential part of Muslim life. In pre-Islamic days, the Holy City of Makka was the centre of commercial activities. It was indeed the annual market there that provided the Prophet Muhammad ﷺ the forum for conveying Islam.

The early Muslims were not only engaged in trade but went to distant lands in connection with business. Islam in fact reached East and West Africa and East Asia through traders. Muslims are encouraged to undertake work in general, and trade and commerce in particular. The Prophet Muhammad ﷺ was himself engaged in this profession before he became a prophet and was a successful businessman, known for his integrity in all of his affairs, for which he was given the name 'Al-Ameen — the Trustworthy'.

I hope this book motivates every aspiring entrepreneur to make a positive difference to the whole of humanity.